C S B
S C R I P T U R E
N O T E B O O K

Proverbs

Read. Reflect. Respond.

CHRISTIAN STANDARD BIBLE® | HOLMAN® BIBLES

Lindsey

May you find love and
guidence from Gods love.
His words of wisdom will
Bless you.
all my love
momma #2

PROVERBS

The Purpose of Proverbs

1 The proverbs of Solomon son of David, king of Israel:
² For learning wisdom and discipline;
for understanding insightful sayings;
³ for receiving prudent instruction
in righteousness, justice, and integrity;
⁴ for teaching shrewdness to the inexperienced,
knowledge and discretion to a young man —
⁵ let a wise person listen and increase learning,
and let a discerning person obtain guidance —
⁶ for understanding a proverb or a parable,
the words of the wise, and their riddles.

⁷ The fear of the LORD
is the beginning of knowledge;
fools despise wisdom and discipline.

Avoid the Path of the Violent

⁸ Listen, my son, to your father's instruction,
and don't reject your mother's teaching,
⁹ for they will be a garland of favor on your head
and pendants around your neck.
¹⁰ My son, if sinners entice you,
don't be persuaded.
¹¹ If they say — "Come with us!
Let's set an ambush and kill someone.
Let's attack some innocent person just for fun!
¹² Let's swallow them alive, like Sheol,
whole, like those who go down to the Pit.
¹³ We'll find all kinds of valuable property
and fill our houses with plunder.
¹⁴ Throw in your lot with us,
and we'll all share the loot" —

¹⁵ my son, don't travel that road with them
   or set foot on their path,
¹⁶ because their feet run toward evil
   and they hurry to shed blood.
¹⁷ It is useless to spread a net
   where any bird can see it,
¹⁸ but they set an ambush to kill themselves;
   they attack their own lives.
¹⁹ Such are the paths of all who make profit dishonestly;
   it takes the lives of those who receive it.

Wisdom's Plea

²⁰ Wisdom calls out in the street;
   she makes her voice heard in the public squares.
²¹ She cries out above the commotion;
   she speaks at the entrance of the city gates:
²² "How long, inexperienced ones, will you love ignorance?
   How long will you mockers enjoy mocking
   and you fools hate knowledge?
²³ If you respond to my warning,
   then I will pour out my spirit on you
   and teach you my words.
²⁴ Since I called out and you refused,
   extended my hand and no one paid attention,
²⁵ since you neglected all my counsel
   and did not accept my correction,
²⁶ I, in turn, will laugh at your calamity.
   I will mock when terror strikes you,
²⁷ when terror strikes you like a storm
   and your calamity comes like a whirlwind,
   when trouble and stress overcome you.
²⁸ Then they will call me, but I won't answer;
   they will search for me, but won't find me.

²⁹ Because they hated knowledge,
   didn't choose to fear the LORD,
³⁰ were not interested in my counsel,
   and rejected all my correction,
³¹ they will eat the fruit of their way
   and be glutted with their own schemes.
³² For the apostasy of the inexperienced will kill them,
   and the complacency of fools will destroy them.
³³ But whoever listens to me will live securely
   and be undisturbed by the dread of danger."

Wisdom's Worth

2 My son, if you accept my words
   and store up my commands within you,
² listening closely to wisdom
   and directing your heart to understanding;
³ furthermore, if you call out to insight
   and lift your voice to understanding,
⁴ if you seek it like silver
   and search for it like hidden treasure,
⁵ then you will understand the fear of the LORD
   and discover the knowledge of God.
⁶ For the LORD gives wisdom;
   from his mouth come knowledge and understanding.
⁷ He stores up success for the upright;
   He is a shield for those who live with integrity
⁸ so that he may guard the paths of justice
   and protect the way of his faithful followers.
⁹ Then you will understand righteousness, justice,
   and integrity — every good path.
¹⁰ For wisdom will enter your heart,
   and knowledge will delight you.
¹¹ Discretion will watch over you,

and understanding will guard you.
¹² It will rescue you from the way of evil —
from anyone who says perverse things,
¹³ from those who abandon the right paths
to walk in ways of darkness,
¹⁴ from those who enjoy doing evil
and celebrate perversion,
¹⁵ whose paths are crooked,
and whose ways are devious.
¹⁶ It will rescue you from a forbidden woman,
from a wayward woman
with her flattering talk,
¹⁷ who abandons the companion of her youth
and forgets the covenant of her God;
¹⁸ for her house sinks down to death
and her ways to the land of the departed spirits.
¹⁹ None return who go to her;
none reach the paths of life.
²⁰ So follow the way of the good,
and keep to the paths of the righteous.
²¹ For the upright will inhabit the land,
and those of integrity will remain in it;
²² but the wicked will be cut off from the land,
and the treacherous ripped out of it.

Trust the LORD

3 My son, don't forget my teaching,
but let your heart keep my commands;
² for they will bring you
many days, a full life, and well-being.
³ Never let loyalty and faithfulness leave you.
Tie them around your neck;
write them on the tablet of your heart.

4 Then you will find favor and high regard
  with God and people.

5 Trust in the LORD with all your heart,
  and do not rely on your own understanding;
6 in all your ways know him,
  and he will make your paths straight.
7 Don't be wise in your own eyes;
  fear the LORD and turn away from evil.
8 This will be healing for your body
  and strengthening for your bones.
9 Honor the LORD with your possessions
  and with the first produce of your entire harvest;
10 then your barns will be completely filled,
  and your vats will overflow with new wine.
11 Do not despise the LORD's instruction, my son,
  and do not loathe his discipline;
12 for the LORD disciplines the one he loves,
  just as a father disciplines the son in whom he delights.

Wisdom Brings Happiness
13 Happy is a man who finds wisdom
  and who acquires understanding,
14 for she is more profitable than silver,
  and her revenue is better than gold.
15 She is more precious than jewels;
  nothing you desire can equal her.
16 Long life is in her right hand;
  in her left, riches and honor.
17 Her ways are pleasant,
  and all her paths, peaceful.
18 She is a tree of life to those who embrace her,
  and those who hold on to her are happy.

19 The LORD founded the earth by wisdom
and established the heavens by understanding.
20 By his knowledge the watery depths broke open,
and the clouds dripped with dew.

21 Maintain sound wisdom and discretion.
My son, don't lose sight of them.
22 They will be life for you
and adornment for your neck.
23 Then you will go safely on your way;
your foot will not stumble.
24 When you lie down, you will not be afraid;
you will lie down, and your sleep will be pleasant.
25 Don't fear sudden danger
or the ruin of the wicked when it comes,
26 for the LORD will be your confidence
and will keep your foot from a snare.

Treat Others Fairly

27 When it is in your power,
don't withhold good from the one to whom it belongs.
28 Don't say to your neighbor, "Go away! Come back later.
I'll give it tomorrow" — when it is there with you.
29 Don't plan any harm against your neighbor,
for he trusts you and lives near you.
30 Don't accuse anyone without cause,
when he has done you no harm.
31 Don't envy a violent man
or choose any of his ways;
32 for the devious are detestable to the LORD,
but he is a friend to the upright.
33 The LORD's curse is on the household of the wicked,
but he blesses the home of the righteous;

34 He mocks those who mock
but gives grace to the humble.
35 The wise will inherit honor,
but he holds up fools to dishonor.

A Father's Example

4 Listen, sons, to a father's discipline,
and pay attention so that you may gain understanding,
2 for I am giving you good instruction.
Don't abandon my teaching.
3 When I was a son with my father,
tender and precious to my mother,
4 he taught me and said,
"Your heart must hold on to my words.
Keep my commands and live.
5 Get wisdom, get understanding;
don't forget or turn away from the words from my mouth.
6 Don't abandon wisdom, and she will watch over you;
love her, and she will guard you.
7 Wisdom is supreme — so get wisdom.
And whatever else you get, get understanding.
8 Cherish her, and she will exalt you;
if you embrace her, she will honor you.
9 She will place a garland of favor on your head;
she will give you a crown of beauty."

Two Ways of Life

10 Listen, my son. Accept my words,
and you will live many years.
11 I am teaching you the way of wisdom;
I am guiding you on straight paths.
12 When you walk, your steps will not be hindered;
when you run, you will not stumble.

13 Hold on to instruction; don't let go.
   Guard it, for it is your life.
14 Keep off the path of the wicked;
   don't proceed on the way of evil ones.
15 Avoid it; don't travel on it.
   Turn away from it, and pass it by.
16 For they can't sleep
   unless they have done what is evil;
   they are robbed of sleep
   unless they make someone stumble.
17 They eat the bread of wickedness
   and drink the wine of violence.
18 The path of the righteous is like the light of dawn,
   shining brighter and brighter until midday.
19 But the way of the wicked is
      like the darkest gloom;
   they don't know what makes them stumble.

The Straight Path

20 My son, pay attention to my words;
   listen closely to my sayings.
21 Don't lose sight of them;
   keep them within your heart.
22 For they are life to those who find them,
   and health to one's whole body.
23 Guard your heart above all else,
   for it is the source of life.
24 Don't let your mouth speak dishonestly,
   and don't let your lips talk deviously.
25 Let your eyes look forward;
   fix your gaze straight ahead.
26 Carefully consider the path for your feet,
   and all your ways will be established.

²⁷ Don't turn to the right or to the left;
   keep your feet away from evil.

Avoid Seduction

5 My son, pay attention to my wisdom;
   listen closely to my understanding
² so that you may maintain discretion
   and your lips safeguard knowledge.
³ Though the lips of the forbidden woman drip honey
   and her words are smoother than oil,
⁴ in the end she's as bitter as wormwood
   and as sharp as a double-edged sword.
⁵ Her feet go down to death;
   her steps head straight for Sheol.
⁶ She doesn't consider the path of life;
   she doesn't know that her ways are unstable.

⁷ So now, sons, listen to me,
   and don't turn away from the words
      from my mouth.
⁸ Keep your way far from her.
   Don't go near the door of her house.
⁹ Otherwise, you will give up your vitality to others
   and your years to someone cruel;
¹⁰ strangers will drain your resources,
   and your hard-earned pay will end up
      in a foreigner's house.
¹¹ At the end of your life, you will lament
   when your physical body has been consumed,
¹² and you will say, "How I hated discipline,
   and how my heart despised correction.
¹³ I didn't obey my teachers
   or listen closely to my instructors.

¹⁴ I am on the verge of complete ruin
before the entire community."

Enjoy Marriage

¹⁵ Drink water from your own cistern,
water flowing from your own well.
¹⁶ Should your springs flow in the streets,
streams in the public squares?
¹⁷ They should be for you alone
and not for you to share with strangers.
¹⁸ Let your fountain be blessed,
and take pleasure in the wife of your youth.
¹⁹ A loving deer, a graceful doe —
let her breasts always satisfy you;
be lost in her love forever.
²⁰ Why, my son, would you lose yourself
with a forbidden woman
or embrace a wayward woman?
²¹ For a man's ways are before the LORD's eyes,
and he considers all his paths.
²² A wicked man's iniquities will trap him;
he will become tangled in the ropes of his own sin.
²³ He will die because there is no discipline,
and be lost because of his great stupidity.

Financial Entanglements

6 My son, if you have put up security for your neighbor
or entered into an agreement with a stranger,
² you have been snared by the words of your mouth —
trapped by the words from your mouth.
³ Do this, then, my son, and free yourself,
for you have put yourself in your neighbor's power:
Go, humble yourself, and plead with your neighbor.

4 Don't give sleep to your eyes
    or slumber to your eyelids.
5 Escape like a gazelle from a hunter,
    like a bird from a hunter's trap.

Laziness
6 Go to the ant, you slacker!
    Observe its ways and become wise.
7 Without leader, administrator, or ruler,
8 it prepares its provisions in summer;
    it gathers its food during harvest.
9 How long will you stay in bed, you slacker?
    When will you get up from your sleep?
10 A little sleep, a little slumber,
    a little folding of the arms to rest,
11 and your poverty will come like a robber,
    your need, like a bandit.

The Malicious Man
12 A worthless person, a wicked man
    goes around speaking dishonestly,
13 winking his eyes, signaling with his feet,
    and gesturing with his fingers.
14 He always plots evil with perversity in his heart;
    he stirs up trouble.
15 Therefore calamity will strike him suddenly;
    he will be shattered instantly, beyond recovery.

What the Lord Hates
16 The Lord hates six things;
    in fact, seven are detestable to him:
17 arrogant eyes, a lying tongue,
    hands that shed innocent blood,

¹⁸ a heart that plots wicked schemes,
feet eager to run to evil,
¹⁹ a lying witness who gives false testimony,
and one who stirs up trouble among brothers.

Warning against Adultery

²⁰ My son, keep your father's command,
and don't reject your mother's teaching.
²¹ Always bind them to your heart;
tie them around your neck.
²² When you walk here and there, they will guide you;
when you lie down, they will watch over you;
when you wake up, they will talk to you.
²³ For a command is a lamp, teaching is a light,
and corrective discipline is the way to life.
²⁴ They will protect you from an evil woman,
from the flattering tongue of a wayward woman.
²⁵ Don't lust in your heart for her beauty
or let her captivate you with her eyelashes.
²⁶ For a prostitute's fee is only a loaf of bread,
but the wife of another man goes after a precious life.
²⁷ Can a man embrace fire
and his clothes not be burned?
²⁸ Can a man walk on burning coals
without scorching his feet?
²⁹ So it is with the one who sleeps with
another man's wife;
no one who touches her will go unpunished.
³⁰ People don't despise the thief if he steals
to satisfy himself when he is hungry.
³¹ Still, if caught, he must pay seven times as much;
he must give up all the wealth in his house.
³² The one who commits adultery lacks sense;

whoever does so destroys himself.
³³ He will get a beating and dishonor,
and his disgrace will never be removed.
³⁴ For jealousy enrages a husband,
and he will show no mercy when he takes revenge.
³⁵ He will not be appeased by anything
or be persuaded by lavish bribes.

7 My son, obey my words,
and treasure my commands.
² Keep my commands and live,
and guard my instructions
as you would the pupil of your eye.
³ Tie them to your fingers;
write them on the tablet of your heart.
⁴ Say to wisdom, "You are my sister,"
and call understanding your relative.
⁵ She will keep you from a forbidden woman,
a wayward woman with her flattering talk.

A Story of Seduction
⁶ At the window of my house
I looked through my lattice.
⁷ I saw among the inexperienced,
I noticed among the youths,
a young man lacking sense.
⁸ Crossing the street near her corner,
he strolled down the road to her house
⁹ at twilight, in the evening,
in the dark of the night.
¹⁰ A woman came to meet him
dressed like a prostitute,
having a hidden agenda.

11 She is loud and defiant;
her feet do not stay at home.

12 Now in the street, now in the squares,
she lurks at every corner.

13 She grabs him and kisses him;
she brazenly says to him,

14 "I've made fellowship offerings;
today I've fulfilled my vows.

15 So I came out to meet you,
to search for you, and I've found you.

16 I've spread coverings on my bed —
richly colored linen from Egypt.

17 I've perfumed my bed
with myrrh, aloes, and cinnamon.

18 Come, let's drink deeply of lovemaking until morning.
Let's feast on each other's love!

19 My husband isn't home;
he went on a long journey.

20 He took a bag of silver with him
and will come home at the time of the full moon."

21 She seduces him with her persistent pleading;
she lures with her flattering talk.

22 He follows her impulsively
like an ox going to the slaughter,
like a deer bounding toward a trap

23 until an arrow pierces its liver,
like a bird darting into a snare —
he doesn't know it will cost him his life.

24 Now, sons, listen to me,
and pay attention to the words from my mouth.

25 Don't let your heart turn aside to her ways;
don't stray onto her paths.

²⁶ For she has brought many down to death;
   her victims are countless.
²⁷ Her house is the road to Sheol,
   descending to the chambers of death.

Wisdom's Appeal

8 Doesn't wisdom call out?
   Doesn't understanding make her voice heard?
² At the heights overlooking the road,
   at the crossroads, she takes her stand.
³ Beside the gates leading into the city,
   at the main entrance, she cries out:
⁴ "People, I call out to you;
   my cry is to the children of Adam.
⁵ Learn to be shrewd, you who are inexperienced;
   develop common sense, you who are foolish.
⁶ Listen, for I speak of noble things,
   and what my lips say is right.
⁷ For my mouth tells the truth,
   and wickedness is detestable to my lips.
⁸ All the words from my mouth are righteous;
   none of them are deceptive or perverse.
⁹ All of them are clear to the perceptive,
   and right to those who discover knowledge.
¹⁰ Accept my instruction instead of silver,
   and knowledge rather than pure gold.
¹¹ For wisdom is better than jewels,
   and nothing desirable can equal it.
¹² I, wisdom, share a home with shrewdness
   and have knowledge and discretion.
¹³ To fear the LORD is to hate evil.
   I hate arrogant pride, evil conduct,
   and perverse speech.

¹⁴ I possess good advice and sound wisdom;
I have understanding and strength.
¹⁵ It is by me that kings reign
and rulers enact just law;
¹⁶ by me, princes lead,
as do nobles and all righteous judges.
¹⁷ I love those who love me,
and those who search for me find me.
¹⁸ With me are riches and honor,
lasting wealth and righteousness.
¹⁹ My fruit is better than solid gold,
and my harvest than pure silver.
²⁰ I walk in the ways of righteousness,
along the paths of justice,
²¹ giving wealth as an inheritance to those who love me,
and filling their treasuries.

²² "The LORD acquired me
at the beginning of his creation,
before his works of long ago.
²³ I was formed before ancient times,
from the beginning, before the earth began.
²⁴ I was born
when there were no watery depths
and no springs filled with water.
²⁵ Before the mountains were established,
prior to the hills, I was given birth —
²⁶ before he made the land, the fields,
or the first soil on earth.
²⁷ I was there when he established the heavens,
when he laid out the horizon on the surface of the ocean,
²⁸ when he placed the skies above,
when the fountains of the ocean gushed out,

²⁹ when he set a limit for the sea
so that the waters would not violate his command,
when he laid out the foundations of the earth.
³⁰ I was a skilled craftsman beside him.
I was his delight every day,
always rejoicing before him.
³¹ I was rejoicing in his inhabited world,
delighting in the children of Adam.

³² "And now, sons, listen to me;
those who keep my ways are happy.
³³ Listen to instruction and be wise;
don't ignore it.
³⁴ Anyone who listens to me is happy,
watching at my doors every day,
waiting by the posts of my doorway.
³⁵ For the one who finds me finds life
and obtains favor from the LORD,
³⁶ but the one who misses me harms himself;
all who hate me love death."

Wisdom versus Foolishness

9 Wisdom has built her house;
she has carved out her seven pillars.
² She has prepared her meat; she has mixed her wine;
she has also set her table.
³ She has sent out her female servants;
she calls out from the highest points of the city:
⁴ "Whoever is inexperienced, enter here!"
To the one who lacks sense, she says,
⁵ "Come, eat my bread,
and drink the wine I have mixed.
⁶ Leave inexperience behind, and you will live;

pursue the way of understanding.
7 The one who corrects a mocker
will bring abuse on himself;
the one who rebukes the wicked will get hurt.
8 Don't rebuke a mocker, or he will hate you;
rebuke the wise, and he will love you.
9 Instruct the wise, and he will be wiser still;
teach the righteous, and he will learn more.

10 "The fear of the Lord is the beginning of wisdom,
and the knowledge of the Holy One is understanding.
11 For by me your days will be many,
and years will be added to your life.
12 If you are wise, you are wise for your own benefit;
if you mock, you alone will bear the consequences."

13 Folly is a rowdy woman;
she is gullible and knows nothing.
14 She sits by the doorway of her house,
on a seat at the highest point of the city,
15 calling to those who pass by,
who go straight ahead on their paths:
16 "Whoever is inexperienced, enter here!"
To the one who lacks sense, she says,
17 "Stolen water is sweet,
and bread eaten secretly is tasty!"
18 But he doesn't know that the departed spirits are there,
that her guests are in the depths of Sheol.

A Collection of Solomon's Proverbs

10 Solomon's proverbs:
A wise son brings joy to his father,
but a foolish son, heartache to his mother.

2 Ill-gotten gains do not profit anyone,
but righteousness rescues from death.

3 The LORD will not let the righteous go hungry,
but he denies the wicked what they crave.

4 Idle hands make one poor,
but diligent hands bring riches.

5 The son who gathers during summer is prudent;
the son who sleeps during harvest is disgraceful.

6 Blessings are on the head of the righteous,
but the mouth of the wicked conceals violence.

7 The remembrance of the righteous
is a blessing,
but the name of the wicked will rot.

8 A wise heart accepts commands,
but foolish lips will be destroyed.

9 The one who lives with integrity lives securely,
but whoever perverts his ways will be found out.

10 A sly wink of the eye causes grief,
and foolish lips will be destroyed.

11 The mouth of the righteous is a fountain of life,
but the mouth of the wicked conceals violence.

12 Hatred stirs up conflicts,
but love covers all offenses.

¹³ Wisdom is found on the lips of the discerning,
but a rod is for the back of the one who lacks sense.

¹⁴ The wise store up knowledge,
but the mouth of the fool hastens destruction.

¹⁵ The wealth of the rich is his fortified city;
the poverty of the poor is their destruction.

¹⁶ The reward of the righteous is life;
the wages of the wicked is punishment.

¹⁷ The one who follows instruction is
on the path to life,
but the one who rejects correction goes astray.

¹⁸ The one who conceals hatred has lying lips,
and whoever spreads slander is a fool.

¹⁹ When there are many words, sin is unavoidable,
but the one who controls his lips is prudent.

²⁰ The tongue of the righteous is pure silver;
the heart of the wicked is of little value.

²¹ The lips of the righteous feed many,
but fools die for lack of sense.

²² The Lord's blessing enriches,
and he adds no painful effort to it.

²³ As shameful conduct is pleasure for a fool,
so wisdom is for a person of understanding.

24 What the wicked dreads will come to him,
but what the righteous desire will be given to them.

25 When the whirlwind passes,
the wicked are no more,
but the righteous are secure forever.

26 Like vinegar to the teeth and smoke to the eyes,
so the slacker is to the one who sends him on an errand.

27 The fear of the LORD prolongs life,
but the years of the wicked are cut short.

28 The hope of the righteous is joy,
but the expectation of the wicked will perish.

29 The way of the LORD is a stronghold for the honorable,
but destruction awaits evildoers.

30 The righteous will never be shaken,
but the wicked will not remain on the earth.

31 The mouth of the righteous produces wisdom,
but a perverse tongue will be cut out.

32 The lips of the righteous know what is appropriate,
but the mouth of the wicked, only what is perverse.

11 Dishonest scales are detestable to the LORD,
but an accurate weight is his delight.

2 When arrogance comes, disgrace follows,
but with humility comes wisdom.

3 The integrity of the upright guides them,
   but the perversity of the treacherous destroys them.

4 Wealth is not profitable on a day of wrath,
   but righteousness rescues from death.

5 The righteousness of the blameless clears his path,
   but the wicked person will fall because of his wickedness.

6 The righteousness of the upright rescues them,
   but the treacherous are trapped by their own desires.

7 When the wicked person dies,
   his expectation comes to nothing,
   and hope placed in wealth vanishes.

8 The righteous one is rescued from trouble;
   in his place, the wicked one goes in.

9 With his mouth the ungodly destroys his neighbor,
   but through knowledge the righteous are rescued.

10 When the righteous thrive, a city rejoices;
    when the wicked die, there is joyful shouting.

11 A city is built up by the blessing of the upright,
    but it is torn down by the mouth of the wicked.

12 Whoever shows contempt for his neighbor lacks sense,
    but a person with understanding keeps silent.

13 A gossip goes around revealing a secret,
    but a trustworthy person keeps a confidence.

¹⁴ Without guidance, a people will fall,
    but with many counselors there is deliverance.

¹⁵ If someone puts up security for a stranger,
    he will suffer for it,
    but the one who hates such agreements
      is protected.

¹⁶ A gracious woman gains honor,
    but violent people gain only riches.

¹⁷ A kind man benefits himself,
    but a cruel person brings ruin on himself.

¹⁸ The wicked person earns an empty wage,
    but the one who sows righteousness, a true reward.

¹⁹ Genuine righteousness leads to life,
    but pursuing evil leads to death.

²⁰ Those with twisted minds are detestable
      to the LORD,
    but those with blameless conduct are his delight.

²¹ Be assured that a wicked person
    will not go unpunished,
    but the offspring of the righteous will escape.

²² A beautiful woman who rejects good sense
    is like a gold ring in a pig's snout.

²³ The desire of the righteous turns out well,
    but the hope of the wicked leads to wrath.

24 One person gives freely,
yet gains more;
another withholds what is right,
only to become poor.

25 A generous person will be enriched,
and the one who gives a drink of water
will receive water.

26 People will curse anyone who hoards grain,
but a blessing will come to the one who sells it.

27 The one who searches for what is good
seeks favor,
but if someone looks for trouble,
it will come to him.

28 Anyone trusting in his riches will fall,
but the righteous will flourish like foliage.

29 The one who brings ruin on his household
will inherit the wind,
and a fool will be a slave
to someone whose heart is wise.

30 The fruit of the righteous is a tree of life,
but a cunning person takes lives.

31 If the righteous will be repaid on earth,
how much more the wicked and sinful.

12 Whoever loves discipline loves knowledge,
but one who hates correction is stupid.

2   One who is good obtains favor from the LORD,
    but he condemns a person who schemes.

3   No one can be made secure by wickedness,
    but the root of the righteous is immovable.

4   A wife of noble character is her husband's crown,
    but a wife who causes shame
    is like rottenness in his bones.

5   The thoughts of the righteous are just,
    but guidance from the wicked is deceitful.

6   The words of the wicked are a deadly ambush,
    but the speech of the upright rescues them.

7   The wicked are overthrown and perish,
    but the house of the righteous will stand.

8   A man is praised for his insight,
    but a twisted mind is despised.

9   Better to be disregarded, yet have a servant,
    than to act important but have no food.

10 The righteous cares about his animal's health,
    but even the merciful acts of the wicked are cruel.

11 The one who works his land will have plenty of food,
    but whoever chases fantasies lacks sense.

12 The wicked desire what evil people have caught,
    but the root of the righteous is productive.

¹³ By rebellious speech an evil person is trapped,
but a righteous person escapes from trouble.

¹⁴ A person will be satisfied with good
by the fruit of his mouth,
and the work of a person's hands
will reward him.

¹⁵ A fool's way is right in his own eyes,
but whoever listens to counsel is wise.

¹⁶ A fool's displeasure is known at once,
but whoever ignores an insult is sensible.

¹⁷ Whoever speaks the truth declares
what is right,
but a false witness speaks deceit.

¹⁸ There is one who speaks rashly,
like a piercing sword;
but the tongue of the wise brings healing.

¹⁹ Truthful lips endure forever,
but a lying tongue, only a moment.

²⁰ Deceit is in the hearts of those who plot evil,
but those who promote peace have joy.

²¹ No disaster overcomes the righteous,
but the wicked are full of misery.

²² Lying lips are detestable to the LORD,
but faithful people are his delight.

²³ A shrewd person conceals knowledge,
but a foolish heart publicizes stupidity.

²⁴ The diligent hand will rule,
but laziness will lead to forced labor.

²⁵ Anxiety in a person's heart weighs it down,
but a good word cheers it up.

²⁶ A righteous person is careful in dealing with his neighbor,
but the ways of the wicked lead them astray.

²⁷ A lazy hunter doesn't roast his game,
but to a diligent person, his wealth is precious.

²⁸ There is life in the path of righteousness,
and in its path there is no death.

13 A wise son responds to his father's discipline,
but a mocker doesn't listen to rebuke.

² From the fruit of his mouth,
a person will enjoy good things,
but treacherous people have an appetite for violence.

³ The one who guards his mouth protects his life;
the one who opens his lips invites his own ruin.

⁴ The slacker craves, yet has nothing,
but the diligent is fully satisfied.

⁵ The righteous hate lying,
but the wicked bring disgust and shame.

⁶ Righteousness guards people of integrity,
but wickedness undermines the sinner.

⁷ One person pretends to be rich but has nothing;
another pretends to be poor but has abundant wealth.

⁸ Riches are a ransom for a person's life,
but a poor person hears no threat.

⁹ The light of the righteous shines brightly,
but the lamp of the wicked is put out.

¹⁰ Arrogance leads to nothing but strife,
but wisdom is gained by those who take advice.

¹¹ Wealth obtained by fraud will dwindle,
but whoever earns it through labor will multiply it.

¹² Hope delayed makes the heart sick,
but desire fulfilled is a tree of life.

¹³ The one who has contempt for instruction will pay
the penalty,
but the one who respects a command will be rewarded.

¹⁴ A wise person's instruction is a fountain of life,
turning people away from the snares of death.

¹⁵ Good sense wins favor,
but the way of the treacherous never changes.

¹⁶ Every sensible person acts knowledgeably,
but a fool displays his stupidity.

¹⁷ A wicked envoy falls into trouble,
but a trustworthy courier brings healing.

¹⁸ Poverty and disgrace come to those
who ignore discipline,
but the one who accepts correction will be honored.

¹⁹ Desire fulfilled is sweet to the taste,
but to turn from evil is detestable to fools.

²⁰ The one who walks with the wise will become wise,
but a companion of fools will suffer harm.

²¹ Disaster pursues sinners,
but good rewards the righteous.

²² A good man leaves an inheritance to his grandchildren,
but the sinner's wealth is stored up for the righteous.

²³ The uncultivated field of the poor yields abundant food,
but without justice, it is swept away.

²⁴ The one who will not use the rod hates his son,
but the one who loves him disciplines him diligently.

²⁵ A righteous person eats until he is satisfied,
but the stomach of the wicked is empty.

14 Every wise woman builds her house,
but a foolish one tears it down with her own hands.

² Whoever lives with integrity fears the LORD,
but the one who is devious in his ways despises him.

3 The proud speech of a fool brings a rod of discipline,
but the lips of the wise protect them.

4 Where there are no oxen, the feeding trough is empty,
but an abundant harvest comes through the strength
of an ox.

5 An honest witness does not deceive,
but a dishonest witness utters lies.

6 A mocker seeks wisdom and doesn't find it,
but knowledge comes easily to the perceptive.

7 Stay away from a foolish person;
you will gain no knowledge from his speech.

8 The sensible person's wisdom is to consider his way,
but the stupidity of fools deceives them.

9 Fools mock at making reparation,
but there is goodwill among the upright.

10 The heart knows its own bitterness,
and no outsider shares in its joy.

11 The house of the wicked will be destroyed,
but the tent of the upright will flourish.

12 There is a way that seems right to a person,
but its end is the way to death.

13 Even in laughter a heart may be sad,
and joy may end in grief.

14 The disloyal one will get what his conduct deserves,
    and a good one, what his deeds deserve.

15 The inexperienced one believes anything,
    but the sensible one watches his steps.

16 A wise person is cautious and turns from evil,
    but a fool is easily angered and is careless.

17 A quick-tempered person acts foolishly,
    and one who schemes is hated.

18 The inexperienced inherit foolishness,
    but the sensible are crowned with knowledge.

19 The evil bow before those who are good,
    and the wicked, at the gates of the righteous.

20 A poor person is hated even by his neighbor,
    but there are many who love the rich.

21 The one who despises his neighbor sins,
    but whoever shows kindness to the poor
       will be happy.

22 Don't those who plan evil go astray?
    But those who plan good find loyalty and faithfulness.

23 There is profit in all hard work,
    but endless talk leads only to poverty.

24 The crown of the wise is their wealth,
    but the foolishness of fools produces foolishness.

25 A truthful witness rescues lives,
   but one who utters lies is deceitful.

26 In the fear of the LORD one has strong confidence
   and his children have a refuge.

27 The fear of the LORD is a fountain of life,
   turning people away from the snares of death.

28 A large population is a king's splendor,
   but a shortage of people is a ruler's devastation.

29 A patient person shows great understanding,
   but a quick-tempered one promotes foolishness.

30 A tranquil heart is life to the body,
   but jealousy is rottenness to the bones.

31 The one who oppresses the poor person insults
      his Maker,
   but one who is kind to the needy honors him.

32 The wicked one is thrown down by his own sin,
   but the righteous one has a refuge in his death.

33 Wisdom resides in the heart of the discerning;
   she is known even among fools.

34 Righteousness exalts a nation,
   but sin is a disgrace to any people.

35 A king favors a prudent servant,
   but his anger falls on a disgraceful one.

15 A gentle answer turns away anger,
but a harsh word stirs up wrath.

2 The tongue of the wise makes knowledge attractive,
but the mouth of fools blurts out foolishness.

3 The eyes of the LORD are everywhere,
observing the wicked and the good.

4 The tongue that heals is a tree of life,
but a devious tongue breaks the spirit.

5 A fool despises his father's discipline,
but a person who accepts correction is sensible.

6 The house of the righteous has great wealth,
but trouble accompanies the income of the wicked.

7 The lips of the wise broadcast knowledge,
but not so the heart of fools.

8 The sacrifice of the wicked is detestable
to the LORD,
but the prayer of the upright is his delight.

9 The LORD detests the way of the wicked,
but he loves the one who pursues righteousness.

10 Discipline is harsh for the one who leaves the path;
the one who hates correction will die.

11 Sheol and Abaddon lie open before the LORD —
how much more, human hearts.

12 A mocker doesn't love one who corrects him;
    he will not consult the wise.

13 A joyful heart makes a face cheerful,
    but a sad heart produces a broken spirit.

14 A discerning mind seeks knowledge,
    but the mouth of fools feeds on foolishness.

15 All the days of the oppressed are miserable,
    but a cheerful heart has a continual feast.

16 Better a little with the fear of the LORD
    than great treasure with turmoil.

17 Better a meal of vegetables where there is love
    than a fattened ox with hatred.

18 A hot-tempered person stirs up conflict,
    but one slow to anger calms strife.

19 A slacker's way is like a thorny hedge,
    but the path of the upright is a highway.

20 A wise son brings joy to his father,
    but a foolish man despises his mother.

21 Foolishness brings joy to one without sense,
    but a person with understanding walks
        a straight path.

22 Plans fail when there is no counsel,
    but with many advisers they succeed.

23 A person takes joy in giving an answer;
and a timely word — how good that is!

24 For the prudent the path of life leads upward,
so that he may avoid going down to Sheol.

25 The LORD tears apart the house of the proud,
but he protects the widow's territory.

26 The LORD detests the plans of the one who is evil,
but pleasant words are pure.

27 The one who profits dishonestly troubles his household,
but the one who hates bribes will live.

28 The mind of the righteous person thinks
    before answering,
but the mouth of the wicked blurts out evil things.

29 The LORD is far from the wicked,
but he hears the prayer of the righteous.

30 Bright eyes cheer the heart;
good news strengthens the bones.

31 One who listens to life-giving rebukes
will be at home among the wise.

32 Anyone who ignores discipline despises himself,
but whoever listens to correction acquires good sense.

33 The fear of the LORD is what wisdom teaches,
and humility comes before honor.

16 The reflections of the heart belong to mankind,
but the answer of the tongue is from the LORD.

2 All a person's ways seem right to him,
but the LORD weighs motives.

3 Commit your activities to the LORD,
and your plans will be established.

4 The LORD has prepared everything for his purpose —
even the wicked for the day of disaster.

5 Everyone with a proud heart is detestable
to the LORD;
be assured, he will not go unpunished.

6 Iniquity is atoned for by loyalty and faithfulness,
and one turns from evil by the fear of the LORD.

7 When a person's ways please the LORD,
he makes even his enemies to be at peace with him.

8 Better a little with righteousness
than great income with injustice.

9 A person's heart plans his way,
but the LORD determines his steps.

10 God's verdict is on the lips of a king;
his mouth should not give an unfair judgment.

11 Honest balances and scales are the LORD's;
all the weights in the bag are his concern.

¹² Wicked behavior is detestable to kings,
   since a throne is established
      through righteousness.

¹³ Righteous lips are a king's delight,
   and he loves one who speaks honestly.

¹⁴ A king's fury is a messenger of death,
   but a wise person appeases it.

¹⁵ When a king's face lights up, there is life;
   his favor is like a cloud with spring rain.

¹⁶ Get wisdom —
   how much better it is than gold!
   And get understanding —
   it is preferable to silver.

¹⁷ The highway of the upright avoids evil;
   the one who guards his way protects his life.

¹⁸ Pride comes before destruction,
   and an arrogant spirit before a fall.

¹⁹ Better to be lowly of spirit with the humble
   than to divide plunder with the proud.

²⁰ The one who understands a matter finds success,
   and the one who trusts in the LORD
      will be happy.

²¹ Anyone with a wise heart is called discerning,
   and pleasant speech increases learning.

²² Insight is a fountain of life for its possessor,
but the discipline of fools is folly.

²³ The heart of a wise person instructs his mouth;
it adds learning to his speech.

²⁴ Pleasant words are a honeycomb:
sweet to the taste and health to the body.

²⁵ There is a way that seems right to a person,
but its end is the way to death.

²⁶ A worker's appetite works for him
because his hunger urges him on.

²⁷ A worthless person digs up evil,
and his speech is like a scorching fire.

²⁸ A contrary person spreads conflict,
and a gossip separates close friends.

²⁹ A violent person lures his neighbor,
leading him on a path that is not good.

³⁰ The one who narrows his eyes
is planning deceptions;
the one who compresses his lips brings about evil.

³¹ Gray hair is a glorious crown;
it is found in the ways of righteousness.

³² Patience is better than power,
and controlling one's emotions, than capturing a city.

³³ The lot is cast into the lap,
but its every decision is from the L ORD.

17 Better a dry crust with peace
than a house full of feasting with strife.

² A prudent servant will rule over a disgraceful son
and share an inheritance among brothers.

³ A crucible for silver, and a smelter for gold,
and the L ORD is the tester of hearts.

⁴ A wicked person listens to malicious talk;
a liar pays attention to a destructive tongue.

⁵ The one who mocks the poor insults his Maker,
and one who rejoices over calamity
will not go unpunished.

⁶ Grandchildren are the crown of the elderly,
and the pride of children is their fathers.

⁷ Eloquent words are not appropriate on a fool's lips;
how much worse are lies for a ruler.

⁸ A bribe seems like a magic stone to its owner;
wherever he turns, he succeeds.

⁹ Whoever conceals an offense promotes love,
but whoever gossips about it separates friends.

¹⁰ A rebuke cuts into a perceptive person
more than a hundred lashes into a fool.

¹¹ An evil person desires only rebellion;
a cruel messenger will be sent against him.

¹² Better for a person to meet a bear robbed
of her cubs
than a fool in his foolishness.

¹³ If anyone returns evil for good,
evil will never depart from his house.

¹⁴ To start a conflict is to release a flood;
stop the dispute before it breaks out.

¹⁵ Acquitting the guilty and condemning the just —
both are detestable to the LORD.

¹⁶ Why does a fool have money in his hand
with no intention of buying wisdom?

¹⁷ A friend loves at all times,
and a brother is born for a difficult time.

¹⁸ One without sense enters an agreement
and puts up security for his friend.

¹⁹ One who loves to offend loves strife;
one who builds a high threshold invites injury.

²⁰ One with a twisted mind will not succeed,
and one with deceitful speech will fall into ruin.

²¹ A man fathers a fool to his own sorrow;
the father of a fool has no joy.

²² A joyful heart is good medicine,
but a broken spirit dries up the bones.

²³ A wicked person secretly takes a bribe
to subvert the course of justice.

²⁴ Wisdom is the focus of the perceptive,
but a fool's eyes roam to the ends of the earth.

²⁵ A foolish son is grief to his father
and bitterness to the one who bore him.

²⁶ It is certainly not good to fine an innocent person
or to beat a noble for his honesty.

²⁷ The one who has knowledge restrains his words,
and one who keeps a cool head
is a person of understanding.

²⁸ Even a fool is considered wise when he keeps silent —
discerning, when he seals his lips.

18 One who isolates himself pursues selfish desires;
he rebels against all sound wisdom.

² A fool does not delight in understanding,
but only wants to show off his opinions.

³ When a wicked person comes, contempt also comes,
and along with dishonor, derision.

⁴ The words of a person's mouth are deep waters,
a flowing river, a fountain of wisdom.

⁵ It is not good to show partiality to the guilty,
  denying an innocent person justice.

⁶ A fool's lips lead to strife,
  and his mouth provokes a beating.

⁷ A fool's mouth is his devastation,
  and his lips are a trap for his life.

⁸ A gossip's words are like choice food
  that goes down to one's innermost being.

⁹ The one who is lazy in his work
  is brother to a vandal.

¹⁰ The name of the LORD is a strong tower;
   the righteous run to it and are protected.

¹¹ The wealth of the rich is his fortified city;
   in his imagination it is like a high wall.

¹² Before his downfall a person's heart is proud,
   but humility comes before honor.

¹³ The one who gives an answer before he listens —
   this is foolishness and disgrace for him.

¹⁴ A person's spirit can endure sickness,
   but who can survive a broken spirit?

¹⁵ The mind of the discerning
      acquires knowledge,
   and the ear of the wise seeks it.

¹⁶ A person's gift opens doors for him
and brings him before the great.

¹⁷ The first to state his case seems right
until another comes and cross-examines him.

¹⁸ Casting the lot ends quarrels
and separates powerful opponents.

¹⁹ An offended brother is harder to reach
than a fortified city,
and quarrels are like the bars
of a fortress.

²⁰ From the fruit of a person's mouth his stomach
is satisfied;
he is filled with the product of his lips.

²¹ Death and life are in the power of the tongue,
and those who love it will eat its fruit.

²² A man who finds a wife finds a good thing
and obtains favor from the LORD.

²³ The poor person pleads,
but the rich one answers roughly.

²⁴ One with many friends may be harmed,
but there is a friend who stays closer
than a brother.

19 Better a poor person who lives with integrity
than someone who has deceitful lips and is a fool.

² Even zeal is not good without knowledge,
and the one who acts hastily sins.

³ A person's own foolishness leads him astray,
yet his heart rages against the LORD.

⁴ Wealth attracts many friends,
but a poor person is separated from his friend.

⁵ A false witness will not go unpunished,
and one who utters lies will not escape.

⁶ Many seek a ruler's favor,
and everyone is a friend of one who gives gifts.

⁷ All the brothers of a poor person hate him;
how much more do his friends
keep their distance from him!
He may pursue them with words,
but they are not there.

⁸ The one who acquires good sense loves himself;
one who safeguards understanding finds success.

⁹ A false witness will not go unpunished,
and one who utters lies perishes.

¹⁰ Luxury is not appropriate for a fool —
how much less for a slave to rule over princes!

¹¹ A person's insight gives him patience,
and his virtue is to overlook an offense.

¹² A king's rage is like the roaring of a lion,
   but his favor is like dew on the grass.

¹³ A foolish son is his father's ruin,
   and a wife's nagging is an endless dripping.

¹⁴ A house and wealth are inherited from fathers,
   but a prudent wife is from the LORD.

¹⁵ Laziness induces deep sleep,
   and a lazy person will go hungry.

¹⁶ The one who keeps commands preserves himself;
   one who disregards his ways will die.

¹⁷ Kindness to the poor is a loan to the LORD,
   and he will give a reward to the lender.

¹⁸ Discipline your son while there is hope;
   don't set your heart on being the cause
      of his death.

¹⁹ A person with intense anger bears the penalty;
   if you rescue him, you'll have to do it again.

²⁰ Listen to counsel and receive instruction
   so that you may be wise later in life.

²¹ Many plans are in a person's heart,
   but the LORD's decree will prevail.

²² What is desirable in a person is his fidelity;
   better to be a poor person than a liar.

²³ The fear of the LORD leads to life;
one will sleep at night without danger.

²⁴ The slacker buries his hand in the bowl;
he doesn't even bring it back to his mouth!

²⁵ Strike a mocker, and the inexperienced learn a lesson;
rebuke the discerning, and he gains knowledge.

²⁶ The one who plunders his father and evicts
his mother
is a disgraceful and shameful son.

²⁷ If you stop listening to correction, my son,
you will stray from the words of knowledge.

²⁸ A worthless witness mocks justice,
and a wicked mouth swallows iniquity.

²⁹ Judgments are prepared for mockers,
and beatings for the backs of fools.

20 Wine is a mocker, beer is a brawler;
whoever goes astray because of them is not wise.

² A king's terrible wrath is like the roaring of a lion;
anyone who provokes him endangers himself.

³ Honor belongs to the person who ends a dispute,
but any fool can get himself into a quarrel.

⁴ The slacker does not plow during planting season;
at harvest time he looks, and there is nothing.

⁵ Counsel in a person's heart is deep water;
but a person of understanding draws it out.

⁶ Many a person proclaims his own loyalty,
but who can find a trustworthy person?

⁷ A righteous person acts with integrity;
his children who come after him
will be happy.

⁸ A king sitting on a throne to judge
separates out all evil with his eyes.

⁹ Who can say, "I have kept my heart pure;
I am cleansed from my sin"?

¹⁰ Differing weights and varying measures —
both are detestable to the LORD.

¹¹ Even a young man is known by his actions —
by whether his behavior is pure and upright.

¹² The hearing ear and the seeing eye —
the LORD made them both.

¹³ Don't love sleep, or you will become poor;
open your eyes, and you'll have enough to eat.

¹⁴ "It's worthless, it's worthless!" the buyer says,
but after he is on his way, he gloats.

¹⁵ There is gold and a multitude of jewels,
but knowledgeable lips are a rare treasure.

¹⁶ Take his garment,
for he has put up security for a stranger;
get collateral if it is for foreigners.

¹⁷ Food gained by fraud is sweet to a person,
but afterward his mouth is full of gravel.

¹⁸ Finalize plans with counsel,
and wage war with sound guidance.

¹⁹ The one who reveals secrets is
a constant gossip;
avoid someone with a big mouth.

²⁰ Whoever curses his father or mother —
his lamp will go out in deep darkness.

²¹ An inheritance gained prematurely
will not be blessed ultimately.

²² Don't say, "I will avenge this evil!"
Wait on the LORD, and he will rescue you.

²³ Differing weights are detestable to the LORD,
and dishonest scales are unfair.

²⁴ Even a courageous person's steps are determined
by the LORD,
so how can anyone understand his own way?

²⁵ It is a trap for anyone to dedicate
something rashly
and later to reconsider his vows.

²⁶ A wise king separates out the wicked
and drives the threshing wheel over them.

²⁷ The LORD's lamp sheds light on a person's life,
searching the innermost parts.

²⁸ Loyalty and faithfulness guard a king;
through loyalty he maintains his throne.

²⁹ The glory of young men is their strength,
and the splendor of old men is gray hair.

³⁰ Lashes and wounds purge away evil,
and beatings cleanse the innermost parts.

21 A king's heart is like channeled water
in the LORD's hand:
He directs it wherever he chooses.

² All a person's ways seem right to him,
but the LORD weighs hearts.

³ Doing what is righteous and just
is more acceptable to the LORD than sacrifice.

⁴ The lamp that guides the wicked —
haughty eyes and an arrogant heart — is sin.

⁵ The plans of the diligent certainly lead to profit,
but anyone who is reckless certainly becomes poor.

⁶ Making a fortune through a lying tongue
is a vanishing mist, a pursuit of death.

7 The violence of the wicked sweeps them away
because they refuse to act justly.

8 A guilty one's conduct is crooked,
but the behavior of the innocent is upright.

9 Better to live on the corner of a roof
than to share a house with a nagging wife.

10 A wicked person desires evil;
he has no consideration for his neighbor.

11 When a mocker is punished,
the inexperienced become wiser;
when one teaches a wise man,
he acquires knowledge.

12 The Righteous One considers the house
of the wicked;
he brings the wicked to ruin.

13 The one who shuts his ears to the cry of the poor
will himself also call out and not be answered.

14 A secret gift soothes anger,
and a covert bribe, fierce rage.

15 Justice executed is a joy to the righteous
but a terror to evildoers.

16 The person who strays from the way of prudence
will come to rest in the assembly of
the departed spirits.

¹⁷ The one who loves pleasure will become poor;
whoever loves wine and oil will not get rich.

¹⁸ The wicked are a ransom for the righteous,
and the treacherous, for the upright.

¹⁹ Better to live in a wilderness
than with a nagging and hot-tempered wife.

²⁰ Precious treasure and oil are in the dwelling of
a wise person,
but a fool consumes them.

²¹ The one who pursues righteousness and faithful love
will find life, righteousness, and honor.

²² A wise person went up against a city of warriors
and brought down its secure fortress.

²³ The one who guards his mouth and tongue
keeps himself out of trouble.

²⁴ The arrogant and proud person, named "Mocker,"
acts with excessive arrogance.

²⁵ A slacker's craving will kill him
because his hands refuse to work.
²⁶ He is filled with craving all day long,
but the righteous give and don't hold back.

²⁷ The sacrifice of a wicked person is detestable —
how much more so
when he brings it with ulterior motives!

²⁸ A lying witness will perish,
but the one who listens will speak successfully.

²⁹ A wicked person puts on a bold face,
but the upright one considers his way.

³⁰ No wisdom, no understanding, and no counsel
will prevail against the LORD.

³¹ A horse is prepared for the day of battle,
but victory comes from the LORD.

22 A good name is to be chosen over great wealth;
favor is better than silver and gold.

² Rich and poor have this in common:
the LORD makes them all.

³ A sensible person sees danger and takes cover,
but the inexperienced keep going and are punished.

⁴ Humility, the fear of the LORD,
results in wealth, honor, and life.

⁵ There are thorns and snares on the way
of the crooked;
the one who guards himself stays far from them.

⁶ Start a youth out on his way;
even when he grows old he will not depart from it.

⁷ The rich rule over the poor,
and the borrower is a slave to the lender.

⁸ The one who sows injustice will reap disaster,
and the rod of his fury will be destroyed.

⁹ A generous person will be blessed,
for he shares his food with the poor.

¹⁰ Drive out a mocker, and conflict goes too;
then quarreling and dishonor will cease.

¹¹ The one who loves a pure heart
and gracious lips — the king is his friend.

¹² The Lord's eyes keep watch over knowledge,
but he overthrows the words of the treacherous.

¹³ The slacker says, "There's a lion outside!
I'll be killed in the public square!"

¹⁴ The mouth of the forbidden woman is a deep pit;
a man cursed by the Lord will fall into it.

¹⁵ Foolishness is bound to the heart of a youth;
a rod of discipline will separate it from him.

¹⁶ Oppressing the poor to enrich oneself,
and giving to the rich — both lead only to poverty.

Words of the Wise
¹⁷ Listen closely, pay attention to the words
of the wise,
and apply your mind to my knowledge.
¹⁸ For it is pleasing if you keep them within you
and if they are constantly on your lips.

¹⁹ I have instructed you today — even you —
so that your confidence may be in the LORD.
²⁰ Haven't I written for you thirty sayings
about counsel and knowledge,
²¹ in order to teach you true and reliable words,
so that you may give a dependable report
to those who sent you?

²² Don't rob a poor person because he is poor,
and don't crush the oppressed at the city gate,
²³ for the LORD will champion their cause
and will plunder those who plunder them.

²⁴ Don't make friends with an angry person,
and don't be a companion of a hot-tempered one,
²⁵ or you will learn his ways
and entangle yourself in a snare.

²⁶ Don't be one of those who enter agreements,
who put up security for loans.
²⁷ If you have nothing with which to pay,
even your bed will be taken from under you.

²⁸ Don't move an ancient boundary marker
that your ancestors set up.

²⁹ Do you see a person skilled in his work?
He will stand in the presence of kings.
He will not stand in the presence
of the unknown.

23 When you sit down to dine with a ruler,
consider carefully what is before you,

² and put a knife to your throat
if you have a big appetite;
³ don't desire his choice food,
for that food is deceptive.

⁴ Don't wear yourself out to get rich;
because you know better, stop!
⁵ As soon as your eyes fly to it, it disappears,
for it makes wings for itself
and flies like an eagle to the sky.

⁶ Don't eat a stingy person's bread,
and don't desire his choice food,
⁷ for it's like someone calculating inwardly.
"Eat and drink," he says to you,
but his heart is not with you.
⁸ You will vomit the little you've eaten
and waste your pleasant words.

⁹ Don't speak to a fool,
for he will despise the insight of your words.

¹⁰ Don't move an ancient boundary marker,
and don't encroach on the fields
of the fatherless,
¹¹ for their Redeemer is strong,
and he will champion their cause against you.

¹² Apply yourself to discipline
and listen to words of knowledge.

¹³ Don't withhold discipline from a youth;
if you punish him with a rod, he will not die.

14 Punish him with a rod,
   and you will rescue his life from Sheol.

15 My son, if your heart is wise,
   my heart will indeed rejoice.
16 My innermost being will celebrate
   when your lips say what is right.

17 Don't let your heart envy sinners;
   instead, always fear the LORD.
18 For then you will have a future,
   and your hope will not be dashed.

19 Listen, my son, and be wise;
   keep your mind on the right course.
20 Don't associate with those who drink too much wine
   or with those who gorge themselves on meat.
21 For the drunkard and the glutton will become poor,
   and grogginess will clothe them in rags.

22 Listen to your father who gave you life,
   and don't despise your mother when she is old.
23 Buy — and do not sell — truth,
   wisdom, instruction, and understanding.
24 The father of a righteous son will rejoice greatly,
   and one who fathers a wise son will delight in him.
25 Let your father and mother have joy,
   and let her who gave birth to you rejoice.

26 My son, give me your heart,
   and let your eyes observe my ways.
27 For a prostitute is a deep pit,
   and a wayward woman is a narrow well;

²⁸ indeed, she sets an ambush like a robber
and increases the number
   of unfaithful people.

²⁹ Who has woe? Who has sorrow?
Who has conflicts? Who has complaints?
Who has wounds for no reason?
Who has red eyes?
³⁰ Those who linger over wine;
those who go looking for mixed wine.
³¹ Don't gaze at wine because it is red,
because it gleams in the cup
and goes down smoothly.
³² In the end it bites like a snake
and stings like a viper.
³³ Your eyes will see strange things,
and you will say absurd things.
³⁴ You'll be like someone sleeping out at sea
or lying down on the top of a ship's mast.
³⁵ "They struck me, but I feel no pain!
They beat me, but I didn't know it!
When will I wake up?
I'll look for another drink."

24 Don't envy the evil
or desire to be with them,
² for their hearts plan violence,
and their words stir up trouble.

³ A house is built by wisdom,
and it is established by understanding;
⁴ by knowledge the rooms are filled
with every precious and beautiful treasure.

⁵ A wise warrior is better than a strong one,
and a man of knowledge than one of strength;
⁶ for you should wage war
with sound guidance —
victory comes with many counselors.

⁷ Wisdom is inaccessible to a fool;
he does not open his mouth at the city gate.

⁸ The one who plots evil
will be called a schemer.
⁹ A foolish scheme is sin,
and a mocker is detestable to people.

¹⁰ If you do nothing in a difficult time,
your strength is limited.
¹¹ Rescue those being taken off to death,
and save those stumbling toward slaughter.
¹² If you say, "But we didn't know about this,"
won't he who weighs hearts consider it?
Won't he who protects your life know?
Won't he repay a person according to
his work?

¹³ Eat honey, my son, for it is good,
and the honeycomb is sweet to your palate;
¹⁴ realize that wisdom is the same for you.
If you find it, you will have a future,
and your hope will never fade.

¹⁵ Don't set an ambush, you wicked one,
at the camp of the righteous man;
don't destroy his dwelling.

16 Though a righteous person falls seven times,
  he will get up,
  but the wicked will stumble into ruin.

17 Don't gloat when your enemy falls,
  and don't let your heart rejoice when he stumbles,
18 or the LORD will see, be displeased,
  and turn his wrath away from him.

19 Don't be agitated by evildoers,
  and don't envy the wicked.
20 For the evil have no future;
  the lamp of the wicked will be put out.

21 My son, fear the LORD, as well as the king,
  and don't associate with rebels,
22 for destruction will come suddenly from them;
  who knows what distress these two can bring?

23 These sayings also belong to the wise:

  It is not good to show partiality in judgment.
24 Whoever says to the guilty, "You are innocent" —
  peoples will curse him, and nations
    will denounce him;
25 but it will go well with those who convict the guilty,
  and a generous blessing will come to them.

26 He who gives an honest answer
  gives a kiss on the lips.

27 Complete your outdoor work, and prepare your field;
  afterward, build your house.

²⁸ Don't testify against your neighbor without cause.
Don't deceive with your lips.
²⁹ Don't say, "I'll do to him what he did to me;
I'll repay the man for what he has done."

³⁰ I went by the field of a slacker
and by the vineyard of one lacking sense.
³¹ Thistles had come up everywhere,
weeds covered the ground,
and the stone wall was ruined.
³² I saw, and took it to heart;
I looked, and received instruction:
³³ a little sleep, a little slumber,
a little folding of the arms to rest,
³⁴ and your poverty will come like a robber,
and your need, like a bandit.

Hezekiah's Collection

25 These too are proverbs of Solomon,
which the men of King Hezekiah of Judah copied.

² It is the glory of God to conceal a matter
and the glory of kings to investigate a matter.
³ As the heavens are high and the earth is deep,
so the hearts of kings cannot be investigated.

⁴ Remove impurities from silver,
and material will be produced for a silversmith.
⁵ Remove the wicked from the king's presence,
and his throne will be established in righteousness.

⁶ Don't boast about yourself before the king,
and don't stand in the place of the great;

⁷ for it is better for him to say to you, "Come up here!"
than to demote you in plain view of a noble.

⁸ Don't take a matter to court hastily.
Otherwise, what will you do afterward
if your opponent humiliates you?
⁹ Make your case with your opponent
without revealing another's secret;
¹⁰ otherwise, the one who hears will disgrace you,
and you'll never live it down.

¹¹ A word spoken at the right time
is like gold apples in silver settings.
¹² A wise correction to a receptive ear
is like a gold ring or an ornament of gold.

¹³ To those who send him, a trustworthy envoy
is like the coolness of snow on a harvest day;
he refreshes the life of his masters.

¹⁴ The one who boasts about a gift that does not exist
is like clouds and wind without rain.
¹⁵ A ruler can be persuaded through patience,
and a gentle tongue can break a bone.
¹⁶ If you find honey, eat only what you need;
otherwise, you'll get sick from it and vomit.
¹⁷ Seldom set foot in your neighbor's house;
otherwise, he'll get sick of you and hate you.

¹⁸ A person giving false testimony against his neighbor
is like a club, a sword, or a sharp arrow.
¹⁹ Trusting an unreliable person in a difficult time
is like a rotten tooth or a faltering foot.

20 Singing songs to a troubled heart
   is like taking off clothing on a cold day
   or like pouring vinegar on soda.

21 If your enemy is hungry, give him food to eat,
   and if he is thirsty, give him water to drink,
22 for you will heap burning coals on his head,
   and the LORD will reward you.

23 The north wind produces rain,
   and a backbiting tongue, angry looks.

24 Better to live on the corner of a roof
   than to share a house with a nagging wife.

25 Good news from a distant land
   is like cold water to a parched throat.

26 A righteous person who yields
      to the wicked
   is like a muddied spring or a polluted well.

27 It is not good to eat too much honey
   or to seek glory after glory.

28 A person who does not control his temper
   is like a city whose wall is broken down.

26 Like snow in summer and rain at harvest,
honor is inappropriate for a fool.

2 Like a flitting sparrow or a fluttering swallow,
  an undeserved curse goes nowhere.

3 A whip for the horse, a bridle for the donkey,
and a rod for the backs of fools.
4 Don't answer a fool according to his foolishness
or you'll be like him yourself.
5 Answer a fool according to his foolishness
or he'll become wise in his own eyes.
6 The one who sends a message by a fool's hand
cuts off his own feet and drinks violence.
7 A proverb in the mouth of a fool
is like lame legs that hang limp.
8 Giving honor to a fool
is like binding a stone in a sling.
9 A proverb in the mouth of a fool
is like a stick with thorns,
brandished by the hand of a drunkard.
10 The one who hires a fool or who hires
those passing by
is like an archer who wounds everyone
indiscriminately.
11 As a dog returns to its vomit,
so also a fool repeats his foolishness.
12 Do you see a person who is wise
in his own eyes?
There is more hope for a fool than for him.

13 The slacker says, "There's a lion in the road —
a lion in the public square!"
14 A door turns on its hinges,
and a slacker, on his bed.
15 The slacker buries his hand in the bowl;
he is too weary to bring it to his mouth!
16 In his own eyes, a slacker is wiser
than seven who can answer sensibly.

¹⁷ A person who is passing by and meddles in a quarrel
    that's not his
  is like one who grabs a dog by the ears.
¹⁸ Like a madman who throws flaming darts
    and deadly arrows,
¹⁹ so is the person who deceives his neighbor
  and says, "I was only joking!"

²⁰ Without wood, fire goes out;
  without a gossip, conflict dies down.
²¹ As charcoal for embers and wood for fire,
  so is a quarrelsome person for kindling strife.
²² A gossip's words are like choice food
  that goes down to one's innermost being.

²³ Smooth lips with an evil heart
  are like glaze on an earthen vessel.
²⁴ A hateful person disguises himself
    with his speech
  and harbors deceit within.
²⁵ When he speaks graciously, don't believe him,
  for there are seven detestable things in his heart.
²⁶ Though his hatred is concealed by deception,
  his evil will be revealed in the assembly.
²⁷ The one who digs a pit will fall into it,
  and whoever rolls a stone —
  it will come back on him.
²⁸ A lying tongue hates those it crushes,
  and a flattering mouth causes ruin.

27 Don't boast about tomorrow,
  for you don't know what a day
  might bring.

2 Let another praise you, and not your own mouth —
a stranger, and not your own lips.

3 A stone is heavy, and sand a burden,
but aggravation from a fool outweighs them both.

4 Fury is cruel, and anger a flood,
but who can withstand jealousy?

5 Better an open reprimand
than concealed love.

6 The wounds of a friend are trustworthy,
but the kisses of an enemy are excessive.

7 A person who is full tramples on a honeycomb,
but to a hungry person, any bitter thing is sweet.

8 Anyone wandering from his home
is like a bird wandering from its nest.

9 Oil and incense bring joy to the heart,
and the sweetness of a friend is better
than self-counsel.

10 Don't abandon your friend or your father's friend,
and don't go to your brother's house
in your time of calamity;
better a neighbor nearby than a brother
far away.

11 Be wise, my son, and bring my heart joy,
so that I can answer anyone who taunts me.

¹² A sensible person sees danger and takes cover;
   the inexperienced keep going
      and are punished.

¹³ Take his garment,
   for he has put up security for a stranger;
   get collateral if it is for foreigners.

¹⁴ If one blesses his neighbor
   with a loud voice early in the morning,
   it will be counted as a curse to him.

¹⁵ An endless dripping on a rainy day
   and a nagging wife are alike;
¹⁶ the one who controls her controls the wind
   and grasps oil with his right hand.

¹⁷ Iron sharpens iron,
   and one person sharpens another.

¹⁸ Whoever tends a fig tree will eat its fruit,
   and whoever looks after his master
      will be honored.

¹⁹ As water reflects the face,
   so the heart reflects the person.

²⁰ Sheol and Abaddon are never satisfied,
   and people's eyes are never satisfied.

²¹ As a crucible refines silver,
   and a smelter refines gold,
   so a person should refine his praise.

²² Though you grind a fool
in a mortar with a pestle along with grain,
you will not separate his foolishness from him.

²³ Know well the condition of your flock,
and pay attention to your herds,
²⁴ for wealth is not forever;
not even a crown lasts for all time.
²⁵ When hay is removed and new growth appears
and the grain from the hills is gathered in,
²⁶ lambs will provide your clothing,
and goats, the price of a field;
²⁷ there will be enough goat's milk for your food —
food for your household
and nourishment for your female servants.

28 The wicked flee when no one is pursuing them,
but the righteous are as bold as a lion.

² When a land is in rebellion, it has many rulers,
but with a discerning and knowledgeable person,
it endures.

³ A destitute leader who oppresses the poor
is like a driving rain that leaves no food.

⁴ Those who reject the law praise the wicked,
but those who keep the law pit themselves
against them.

⁵ The evil do not understand justice,
but those who seek the Lord
understand everything.

6 Better the poor person who lives with integrity
than the rich one who distorts right and wrong.

7 A discerning son keeps the law,
but a companion of gluttons humiliates his father.

8 Whoever increases his wealth
through excessive interest
collects it for one who is kind to the poor.

9 Anyone who turns his ear away from hearing the law—
even his prayer is detestable.

10 The one who leads the upright into an evil way
will fall into his own pit,
but the blameless will inherit what is good.

11 A rich person is wise in his own eyes,
but a poor one who has discernment
sees through him.

12 When the righteous triumph,
there is great rejoicing,
but when the wicked come to power,
people hide.

13 The one who conceals his sins
will not prosper,
but whoever confesses and renounces them
will find mercy.

14 Happy is the one who is always reverent,
but one who hardens his heart falls into trouble.

¹⁵ A wicked ruler over a helpless people
is like a roaring lion or a charging bear.

¹⁶ A leader who lacks understanding
is very oppressive,
but one who hates dishonest profit
prolongs his life.

¹⁷ Someone burdened by bloodguilt
will be a fugitive until death.
Let no one help him.

¹⁸ The one who lives with integrity will be helped,
but one who distorts right and wrong
will suddenly fall.

¹⁹ The one who works his land
will have plenty of food,
but whoever chases fantasies
will have his fill of poverty.

²⁰ A faithful person will have many blessings,
but one in a hurry to get rich
will not go unpunished.

²¹ It is not good to show partiality —
yet even a courageous person may sin for a piece
of bread.

²² A greedy one is in a hurry for wealth;
he doesn't know that poverty will come to him.

23 One who rebukes a person will later find
   more favor
than one who flatters with his tongue.

24 The one who robs his father or mother
and says, "That's no sin,"
is a companion to a person who destroys.

25 A greedy person stirs up conflict,
but whoever trusts in the LORD will prosper.

26 The one who trusts in himself is a fool,
but one who walks in wisdom will be safe.

27 The one who gives to the poor
will not be in need,
but one who turns his eyes away
will receive many curses.

28 When the wicked come to power,
people hide,
but when they are destroyed,
the righteous flourish.

29 One who becomes stiff-necked,
after many reprimands
will be shattered instantly —
beyond recovery.

2 When the righteous flourish,
   the people rejoice,
but when the wicked rule, people groan.

3   A man who loves wisdom brings joy
    to his father,
but one who consorts with prostitutes
    destroys his wealth.

4   By justice a king brings stability to a land,
but a person who demands "contributions"
    demolishes it.

5   A person who flatters his neighbor
spreads a net for his feet.

6   An evil person is caught by sin,
but the righteous one sings and rejoices.

7   The righteous person knows the rights of the poor,
but the wicked one does not understand these concerns.

8   Mockers inflame a city,
but the wise turn away anger.

9   If a wise person goes to court with a fool,
there will be ranting and raving but no resolution.

10 Bloodthirsty men hate an honest person,
but the upright care about him.

11 A fool gives full vent to his anger,
but a wise person holds it in check.

12 If a ruler listens to lies,
all his officials will be wicked.

¹³ The poor and the oppressor have this in common:
the LORD gives light to the eyes of both.

¹⁴ A king who judges the poor with fairness —
his throne will be established forever.

¹⁵ A rod of correction imparts wisdom,
but a youth left to himself
is a disgrace to his mother.

¹⁶ When the wicked increase, rebellion increases,
but the righteous will see their downfall.

¹⁷ Discipline your child, and it will bring you
peace of mind
and give you delight.

¹⁸ Without revelation people run wild,
but one who follows divine instruction
will be happy.

¹⁹ A servant cannot be disciplined by words;
though he understands, he doesn't respond.

²⁰ Do you see someone who speaks too soon?
There is more hope for a fool than for him.

²¹ A servant pampered from his youth
will become arrogant later on.

²² An angry person stirs up conflict,
and a hot-tempered one
increases rebellion.

²³ A person's pride will humble him,
but a humble spirit will gain honor.

²⁴ To be a thief's partner is to hate oneself;
he hears the curse but will not testify.

²⁵ The fear of mankind is a snare,
but the one who trusts in the LORD is protected.

²⁶ Many desire a ruler's favor,
but a person receives justice from the LORD.

²⁷ An unjust person is detestable to the righteous,
and one whose way is upright
is detestable to the wicked.

The Words of Agur

30 The words of Agur son of Jakeh.
The pronouncement.

The man's oration to Ithiel, to Ithiel and Ucal:

² I am more stupid than any other person,
and I lack a human's ability to understand.
³ I have not gained wisdom,
and I have no knowledge of the Holy One.
⁴ Who has gone up to heaven and come down?
Who has gathered the wind in his hands?
Who has bound up the waters in a cloak?
Who has established all the ends of the earth?
What is his name,
and what is the name of his son —
if you know?

⁵ Every word of God is pure;
  he is a shield to those who take refuge in him.
⁶ Don't add to his words,
  or he will rebuke you, and you will be proved a liar.

⁷ Two things I ask of you;
  don't deny them to me before I die:
⁸ Keep falsehood and deceitful words far from me.
  Give me neither poverty nor wealth;
  feed me with the food I need.
⁹ Otherwise, I might have too much
  and deny you, saying, "Who is the LORD?"
  or I might have nothing and steal,
  profaning the name of my God.

¹⁰ Don't slander a servant to his master
  or he will curse you, and you will become guilty.

¹¹ There is a generation that curses its father
  and does not bless its mother.
¹² There is a generation that is pure
    in its own eyes,
  yet is not washed from its filth.
¹³ There is a generation — how haughty its eyes
  and pretentious its looks.
¹⁴ There is a generation whose teeth are swords,
  whose fangs are knives,
  devouring the oppressed from the land
  and the needy from among mankind.

¹⁵ The leech has two daughters: "Give, Give!"
  Three things are never satisfied;
  four never say, "Enough!":

16 Sheol; a childless womb;
    earth, which is never satisfied with water;
    and fire, which never says, "Enough!"

17 As for the eye that ridicules a father
    and despises obedience to a mother,
    may ravens of the valley pluck it out
    and young vultures eat it.

18 Three things are too wondrous for me;
    four I can't understand:
19 the way of an eagle in the sky,
    the way of a snake on a rock,
    the way of a ship at sea,
    and the way of a man with a young woman.

20 This is the way of an adulteress:
    she eats and wipes her mouth
    and says, "I've done nothing wrong."

21 The earth trembles under three things;
    it cannot bear up under four:
22 a servant when he becomes king,
    a fool when he is stuffed with food,
23 an unloved woman when she marries,
    and a servant girl when she ousts her queen.

24 Four things on earth are small,
    yet they are extremely wise:
25 ants are not a strong people,
    yet they store up their food in the summer;
26 hyraxes are not a mighty people,
    yet they make their homes in the cliffs;

²⁷ locusts have no king,
  yet all of them march in ranks;
²⁸ a lizard can be caught in your hands,
  yet it lives in kings' palaces.

²⁹ Three things are stately in their stride;
  four are stately in their walk:
³⁰ a lion, which is mightiest among beasts
  and doesn't retreat before anything;
³¹ a strutting rooster; a goat;
  and a king at the head of his army.

³² If you have been foolish by exalting yourself
  or if you've been scheming,
  put your hand over your mouth.
³³ For the churning of milk produces butter,
  and twisting a nose draws blood,
  and stirring up anger produces strife.

The Words of Lemuel

31 The words of King Lemuel,
  a pronouncement that his mother taught him:

² What should I say, my son?
  What, son of my womb?
  What, son of my vows?
³ Don't spend your energy on women
  or your efforts on those who destroy kings.
⁴ It is not for kings, Lemuel,
  it is not for kings to drink wine
  or for rulers to desire beer.
⁵ Otherwise, he will drink,
  forget what is decreed,

and pervert justice for all the oppressed.
⁶ Give beer to one who is dying
and wine to one whose life is bitter.
⁷ Let him drink so that he can forget his poverty
and remember his trouble no more.
⁸ Speak up for those who have no voice,
for the justice of all who are dispossessed.
⁹ Speak up, judge righteously,
and defend the cause of the oppressed
and needy.

In Praise of a Wife of Noble Character
¹⁰ Who can find a wife of noble character?
She is far more precious than jewels.
¹¹ The heart of her husband trusts in her,
and he will not lack anything good.
¹² She rewards him with good, not evil,
all the days of her life.
¹³ She selects wool and flax
and works with willing hands.
¹⁴ She is like the merchant ships,
bringing her food from far away.
¹⁵ She rises while it is still night
and provides food for her household
and portions for her female servants.
¹⁶ She evaluates a field and buys it;
she plants a vineyard with her earnings.
¹⁷ She draws on her strength
and reveals that her arms are strong.
¹⁸ She sees that her profits are good,
and her lamp never goes out at night.
¹⁹ She extends her hands to the spinning staff,
and her hands hold the spindle.

²⁰ Her hands reach out to the poor,
and she extends her hands to the needy.

²¹ She is not afraid for her household when it snows,
for all in her household are doubly clothed.

²² She makes her own bed coverings;
her clothing is fine linen and purple.

²³ Her husband is known at the city gates,
where he sits among the elders of the land.

²⁴ She makes and sells linen garments;
she delivers belts to the merchants.

²⁵ Strength and honor are her clothing,
and she can laugh at the time to come.

²⁶ Her mouth speaks wisdom,
and loving instruction is on her tongue.

²⁷ She watches over the activities of her household
and is never idle.

²⁸ Her children rise up and call her blessed;
her husband also praises her:

²⁹ "Many women have done noble deeds,
but you surpass them all!"

³⁰ Charm is deceptive and beauty is fleeting,
but a woman who fears the Lord will be praised.

³¹ Give her the reward of her labor,
and let her works praise her at the city gates.